TEAM SPIRIT®

SMART BOOKS FOR YOUNG FANS

THE CHICAGO CUBS

BY
MARK STEWART

NORWOODHOUSE PRESS
CHICAGO, ILLINOIS

Norwood House Press
P.O. Box 316598
Chicago, Illinois 60631

For information regarding Norwood House Press, please visit our website at:
www.norwoodhousepress.com or call 866-565-2900.

All photos courtesy of Getty Images except the following:
Scott Boehm (4), Author's Collection (6, 15, 19, 33, 36, 43 bottom), Baseball Magazine (7),
Black Book Partners Archives (9, 22, 39, 40), SportsChrome (10, 11, 12, 14, 23, 35 bottom),
Plowboy Tobacco (16), Sweet Caporal (17 bottom), Turkey Red (17 top),
Ramly/TTT Tobacco (18), Topps, Inc. (21, 28, 35 top right, 37, 38, 41, 42 bottom, 45),
Goudey Gum Co. (31), Pictorial News Co. (34 bottom left & right), H. Ellis & Co. (34 top),
Chicago Cubs (35 top left), Exhibit Supply Co. (42 top), Old Judge & Gypsy Queen (43 top), Matt Richman (48).
Cover Photo: Brian Kersey/Getty Images

The memorabilia and artifacts pictured in this book are presented for educational and informational purposes,
and come from the collection of the author.

Editor: Mike Kennedy
Designer: Ron Jaffe
Project Management: Black Book Partners, LLC.
Special thanks to Michael Trossman.
Special thanks to Topps, Inc.

Library of Congress Cataloging-in-Publication Data

Stewart, Mark, 1960-
  The Chicago Cubs / by Mark Stewart. -- Library ed.
      p. cm. -- (Team spirit)
  Includes bibliographical references and index.
  Summary: "A Team Spirit Baseball edition featuring the Chicago Cubs that
chronicles the history and accomplishments of the team. Includes access to
the Team Spirit website, which provides additional information, updates and
photos"--Provided by publisher.
    ISBN 978-1-59953-476-3 (libary : alk. paper) -- ISBN 978-1-60357-356-6
(ebook) 1. Chicago Cubs (Baseball team)--History--Juvenile literature. I.
Title.
  GV875.C6S84 2012
  796.357'640977311--dc23
                                              2011047941

Manufactured in the United States of America in North Mankato, Minnesota.
196N—012012

COVER PHOTO: The Cubs celebrate a victory at Wrigley Field.

TABLE OF CONTENTS

ABOUT OUR GLOSSARY

In this book, there may be several words that you are reading for the first time. Some are sports words, some are new vocabulary words, and some are familiar words that are used in an unusual way. All of these words are defined on page 46. Throughout the book, sports words appear in **bold type**. Regular vocabulary words appear in ***bold italic type***.

MEET THE CUBS

In baseball's early days, it took fans only a few minutes to get to the ballpark. Teams played on fields that were built near houses and businesses, and close to bus and train lines. When the home team won, neighbors could hear the crowd roar—from their homes! The Chicago Cubs have been a neighborhood team for more than a century. That is why their fans think of the players as family.

The Cubs play at Wrigley Field. Going there is like entering a time machine. Very little has changed over the years. Ivy still grows on the brick walls in the outfield. The players chat with the fans before games—sometimes during them! The crowd hangs on every pitch.

This book tells the story of the Cubs. The players, the team's ballpark, and the fans are part of baseball history. Every time the Cubs take the field and their fans settle into their seats, they are adding another chapter to the longest-running story in American sports.

The Cubs are a neighborhood team. So the entire "neighborhood" of Chicago celebrates when they win a game.

GLORY DAYS

Sports teams come and go. It is not unusual for a team to change cities, or even go out of business. Baseball fans in Chicago are lucky. They have been rooting for the Cubs since the 1870s. The Chicago club was called the White Stockings in those days. They were one of the best teams in the **National League (NL)**.

The White Stockings won the **pennant** in 1876 and five times from 1880 to 1886. The star of those teams was Cap Anson.

He was one of the league's best hitters and the team's manager for many years. He led the NL in **runs batted in (RBIs)** eight times.

After Anson retired, the Cubs rebuilt their team and won the pennant each season from 1906 to 1908, and again in 1910. They were **World Series** champs in 1907 and 1908. The heart of those clubs was the great infield of Frank Chance,

Johnny Evers, Joe Tinker, and Harry Steinfeldt. The Cubs also had an excellent pitching staff, which was led by Ed Reulbach and Mordecai "Three Finger" Brown. Two of Brown's fingers had been mangled in a childhood accident. His unusual grip made his pitches dart suddenly as they neared home plate.

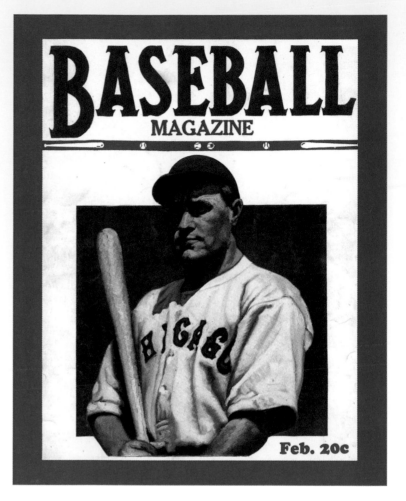

Over the next 35 years, the Cubs had some very good teams and some wonderful players. They were among the NL's best teams during the 1930s and won four pennants from 1929 to 1938. These clubs starred Hack Wilson, Gabby Hartnett, Charlie Grimm, Charlie Root, Kiki Cuyler, Riggs Stephenson, Lon Warneke, Billy Herman, and Stan Hack—all of whom were among the top stars of the time.

LEFT: The 1886 Cubs lost only 34 games.   **ABOVE**: Home run champion Hack Wilson stares out from the cover of *Baseball Magazine*.

In 1945, the Cubs beat the St. Louis Cardinals for the NL pennant. It was their 10th league title in less than 50 years. The Cubs then lost a thrilling World Series to the Detroit Tigers. Though Chicago fans were disappointed, they could hardly wait for the team's next trip to the World Series. It turned out to be a long wait.

Year after year, *decade* after decade, the Cubs failed to win another pennant. They came close many times, but some bit of bad luck always seemed to strike. Great players such as Hank Sauer, Ernie Banks, Ron Santo, Billy Williams, Fergie Jenkins, Bill Madlock, Bruce Sutter, Andre Dawson, Ryne Sandberg, Mark Grace, Greg Maddux, and Sammy Sosa wore the Chicago uniform during this time. Sauer, Banks, Dawson, Sandberg, and Sosa were voted the **Most Valuable Player (MVP)**, but none was able to lead the Cubs back to the World Series.

In many cities, baseball fans would have given up on a team with a history of coming so close so many times. Not Chicago. It is a hard-working city that takes pride in a job well done. As long as the Cubs give their best effort, the players are showered with love. Deep down,

LEFT: Ernie Banks was the team's greatest player.   **ABOVE**: Andre Dawson also won the NL MVP with the Cubs. His award came in 1987.

fans believe the Cubs have a chance to be champions every year. When that championship day comes, they will throw baseball's biggest party.

In the meantime, the Cubs continue to look for the winning formula. They mix experienced stars with young talent. Every season they seem to find new and exciting players. In the early years of the 21st century, the Chicago lineup featured Sosa, Kerry Wood, Mark Prior, and Moises Alou. All had great moments in a Cubs uniform.

LEFT: Mark Prior delivers a pitch. He led the Cubs with 18 victories in 2003.
RIGHT: Starlin Castro stands at the plate. In 2011, he became the youngest Cub to get 200 hits in a season.

In 2003, the Cubs came within a game of returning to the World Series. Unfortunately, they lost in the **National League Championship Series (NLCS)** to the Florida Marlins. Chicago fans were heartbroken, but they didn't lose faith in their team.

By the 2011 season, the names on the scorecard had changed for the Cubs. They included young stars Starlin Castro, Geovany Soto, and Carlos Marmol. Chicago also added *veterans* such as Carlos Zambrano, Alfonso Soriano, Matt Garza, Ryan Dempster, Carlos Pena, Marlon Byrd, and Aramis Ramirez. Each player is like a piece in a puzzle. The Cubs will never stop trying to make every piece a perfect fit.

HOME TURF

Wrigley Field is one of baseball's most beautiful ballparks. It was built in 1914 and originally called Weeghman Park. Almost all of the seats are in the *grandstand* area, so fans sit very close to the players and the field. Unlike other stadiums, the *bleacher seats* in the Cubs' ballpark are the most popular. There's nothing quite like spending an afternoon with the "bleacher bums" of Wrigley Field.

Wrigley Field is rich in *tradition*. The ivy growing on the outfield walls was planted in 1937. The old-time scoreboard also dates back to 1937. From 1914 to 1987, only day games were played at Wrigley Field. Lights were added in 1988, but the Cubs still play more day games than any other team.

BY THE NUMBERS

- *Wrigley Field has 41,160 seats.*
- *The distance from home plate to the left field foul pole is 355 feet.*
- *The distance from home plate to the center field fence is 400 feet.*
- *The distance from home plate to the right field foul pole is 353 feet.*

Wrigley Field's ivy-covered outfield wall and its bleacher seats can be seen in this photo of the stadium.

DRESSED FOR SUCCESS

The Cubs have never been afraid to experiment with their uniforms. In fact, they have worn more than 30 different uniforms since the 1870s. Almost every one has featured some combination of white and blue. Over the years, red became an important team color, too.

The Cubs were the first baseball team to try sleeveless uniforms. They were also the first to try a uniform color that matched the animal they were named after. The little cub first appeared on Chicago uniforms in 1908.

In recent years, the Cubs have worn a number of uniforms that remind fans of their old styles. Their most popular home uniform features blue *pinstripes*. Their cap is also blue, with a red *C* outlined in white.

LEFT: Darwin Barney takes a swing in the Cubs' 2011 home pinstripe uniform.
ABOVE: This photo signed by Billy Williams shows him in a Chicago uniform from the 1960s.

WE WON!

The Cubs have put a lot of good teams on the field over the years, but the last time the club flew a world championship banner was way back in 1908. That season featured one of the craziest endings in history. The Cubs were trying to become the first team to win the World Series twice in a row. First they needed to beat the New York Giants to win the NL pennant.

In a September game between the two teams, New York's Al Bridwell broke a 1–1 tie in the bottom of the ninth inning with a single. At least, that is what the fans thought. But the runner on first base, Fred Merkle, did not bother to touch second base once the winning run had scored.

Johnny Evers fields a grounder. He was the craftiest player of his day.

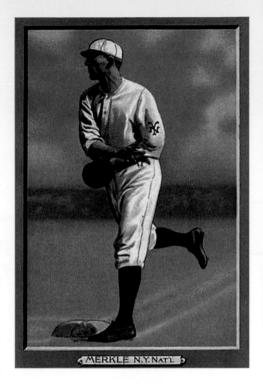

RIGHT: Fred Merkle makes a play in the field. He became more famous for his baserunning mistake.
BELOW: Ray Kroh

As Merkle headed for the locker room, Chicago infielder Johnny Evers noticed what had happened. He knew if he could get the ball and touch second base, the umpires would call a **force-out**, and the winning run would not count. The only problem was that the crowd had swarmed all over the field. The ball was loose among the fans. Shortstop Joe Tinker managed to find the ball, but New York's first base coach snatched it from him and threw it into the stands!

Ray Kroh, a pitcher on the Cubs, found the fan who caught the ball and demanded it back. When the fan refused, Kroh punched him in the nose and took the ball. He handed it to Evers, who made sure umpire Hank O'Day was nearby. When Evers stepped on the base, O'Day stuck his thumb in the air. "Out!" he cried. The league ruled that the game had to be replayed—if necessary.

As luck would have it, the Giants and Cubs finished the season with the same record, 98–55. They met again in New York to replay the game. The Giants took an early lead, but the Cubs came back against New York's great pitcher, Christy Mathewson. Mordecai Brown pitched well for Chicago, and the Cubs hung on to win 4–2.

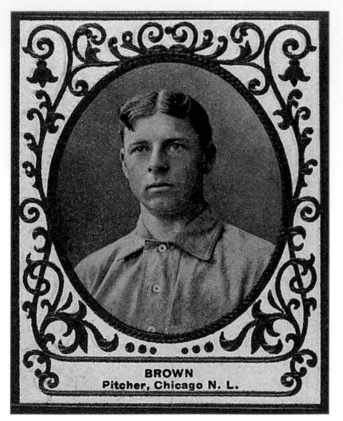

BROWN
Pitcher, Chicago N. L.

Two days later, the Cubs took the field against the Detroit Tigers in the first game of the World Series. If the Chicago pitchers could not stop the great Ty Cobb and his teammates, their marvelous victory would be forgotten. Once again, Brown was the hero. He won Game 1 as a relief pitcher, and then **shut out** the Tigers in Game 4. Orval Overall also won two games. The Cubs won the series four games to one and limited the Tigers to a .203 batting average.

PENNANT WINNERS

WORLD'S
CHAMPIONSHIP
SERIES

OFFICIAL SCORE CARD

DETROIT "TIGERS"
AMERICAN LEAGUE
VS.
CHICAGO "CUBS"
NATIONAL LEAGUE

BENNETT PARK, DETROIT, OCTOBER 1908

H. M. FECHHEIMER, PUBLISHER, 156 WOODWARD AVE.

The Cubs captured the pennant again in 1910, but they lost to the Philadelphia Athletics in the World Series. Chicago returned to the World Series six more times. Each time, the team failed to win it all. The fans who celebrated their team's victory in 1908 never imagined that the Cubs would not win again during the 20th century.

LEFT: Mordecai Brown
ABOVE: This program from the 1908 World Series shows Detroit Tigers star Ty Cobb.

GO-TO GUYS

To be a true star in baseball, you need more than a quick bat and a strong arm. You have to be a "go-to guy"—someone the manager wants on the pitcher's mound or in the batter's box when it matters most. Fans of the Cubs have had a lot to cheer about over the years, including these great stars …

THE PIONEERS

STAN HACK   Third Baseman

• BORN: 12/6/1909   • DIED: 12/15/1979   • PLAYED FOR TEAM: 1932 TO 1947

During the 1930s and 1940s, the face of the Cubs was good-natured Stan Hack. "Smiling Stan" was the NL's top **leadoff hitter**. He was also one of the best defensive players in baseball.

ERNIE BANKS   Shortstop/First Baseman

• BORN: 1/31/1931   • PLAYED FOR TEAM: 1953 TO 1971

Ernie Banks was nicknamed "Mr. Cub." His love of baseball made fans forget that the Cubs were not a very good team while he played for them. Banks hit 512 home runs during his career and was named NL MVP in 1958 and 1959.

BILLY WILLIAMS   Outfielder

- BORN: 6/15/1938   • PLAYED FOR TEAM: 1959 TO 1974

When Billy Williams was on a hot streak, no hitter in baseball was more dangerous. He once went 8-for-8 in a **doubleheader**, and he won the league batting championship in 1972. From 1963 to 1970, Williams played in 1,117 games in a row.

FERGIE JENKINS   Pitcher

- BORN: 12/13/1942   • PLAYED FOR TEAM: 1966 TO 1973 & 1982 TO 1983

Fergie Jenkins was one of the best pitchers in baseball when he played for the Cubs. He had a great fastball and another pitch that dipped out of the strike zone. Jenkins won 20 or more games six seasons in a row for the Cubs.

RON SANTO   Third Baseman

- BORN: 2/25/1940   • DIED: 12/3/2010
- PLAYED FOR TEAM: 1960 TO 1973

Ron Santo was the NL's best all-around third baseman during the 1960s. He was a powerful hitter, a slick fielder, and a *fiery* leader. Santo later announced Cubs games on television and radio. He was voted into the **Hall of Fame** in 2012.

RIGHT: Ron Santo

RYNE SANDBERG   Second Baseman

- BORN: 9/18/1959
- PLAYED FOR TEAM: 1982 TO 1997

Ryne Sandberg was an excellent fielder and a great power hitter. He led the Cubs to the **postseason** for the first time in almost 40 years in 1984. Sandberg was voted the NL MVP that season.

MARK GRACE   First Baseman

- BORN: 6/28/1964
- PLAYED FOR TEAM: 1988 TO 2000

Mark Grace had more hits than any player in baseball during the 1990s. Grace always had a smile on his face, and he was a favorite of Cubs fans.

SAMMY SOSA   Outfielder

- BORN: 11/12/1968
- PLAYED FOR TEAM: 1992 TO 2004

Sammy Sosa was the greatest slugger in team history. He hit 60 or more home runs three times. He also had more than 100 RBIs nine years in a row.

ARAMIS RAMIREZ   Third Baseman

- BORN: 6/25/1978
- PLAYED FOR TEAM: 2003 TO 2011

The Cubs got Aramis Ramirez in a trade with the Pittsburgh Pirates. He soon became the team's top slugger. Ramirez was the first Cub to hit a **grand slam** in a playoff game. He launched three homers in a game twice during the 2004 season.

ALFONSO SORIANO   Outfielder

- BORN: 1/7/1976   • FIRST YEAR WITH TEAM: 2007

Only a handful of players in baseball history combined speed and power the way Alfonso Soriano did. That is why the Cubs signed him in 2007. Soriano earned his pay that season when he hit 14 home runs in September and led Chicago to the **NL Central** crown.

STARLIN CASTRO   Shortstop

- BORN: 3/24/1990   • FIRST YEAR WITH TEAM: 2010

When Starlin Castro joined the Cubs in May of 2010, he became the first **big-leaguer** born in the 1990s. Castro immediately showed fans that he could do it all on the field. In 2011, he became the youngest player ever to lead the NL in hits.

LEFT: Ryne Sandberg   **ABOVE**: Aramis Ramirez

In baseball's early days, it was not unusual for a team's best player to be its manager, too. When the Cubs had "player-managers," good things usually happened. From 1876 to 1910, Al Spalding, Cap Anson, and Frank Chance won eight pennants for the team. In 1932, first baseman Charlie Grimm took over after 99 games and led the Cubs to another pennant.

Chicago has also had some great leaders who served as managers only. Leo Durocher, Don Zimmer, and Dusty Baker all worked in the Cubs' dugout. In 2007, the team hired Lou Piniella. Chicago won the NL Central in his first season. They repeated as NL Central champions in 2008.

One of Chicago's most famous managers was Gabby Hartnett. He was the star of Grimm's team in 1932. Hartnett was a power-hitting catcher. At the time, that was unusual because teams normally relied on their catchers for defense only.

Hartnett was a great hitter, fielder, and team leader. He was named league MVP in 1935. In 1937, Hartnett batted .354. That

Gabby Hartnett watches the action from the dugout. He was one of Chicago's best player-managers.

set the record for highest batting average for a catcher—a record that lasted for 60 years!

In July of 1938, the Cubs decided they needed a new manager. Hartnett agreed to fill Grimm's shoes. Chicago was in third place at the time. By the end of September, they had nearly closed the gap on the first-place Pittsburgh Pirates.

On September 28, Hartnett came to bat in the ninth inning of a 5–5 game against the Pirates. It was getting dark, so the umpires announced this would be the last inning. With two strikes, Hartnett took a mighty cut and launched a homer into the left field stands. Players and fans ran onto the field and circled the bases with their beloved player-manager. The Cubs went on to win the pennant, and Hartnett's blast was forever known as the "Homer in the Gloamin."

ONE GREAT DAY

Everybody who had seen Kerry Wood pitch in the **minor leagues** predicted he would make a good big-leaguer. But no one knew that he would be so good—so soon. When Wood walked to the mound on a gray afternoon in May of 1998 to face the Houston Astros, it was only his fifth start as a member of the Cubs.

Wood had his "good stuff" that day. His fastball was hissing across home plate at almost 100 miles per hour. His curve was bending sharply just as batters started their swings. The first five Astros were helpless against Wood. Each struck out. The next six batters had more luck. They all hit the ball, and one reached first base on a slow grounder. This would be the only hit for the Astros all day.

Wood struck out the next five batters. Each watched strike three sizzle into the catcher's mitt. They knew they had no chance to hit Wood's pitches, so they did not even try. Wood struck out each of the batters he faced in the seventh and eighth innings, giving

That's 20 strikeouts! Kerry Wood gets a hug from Mark Grace and a pat on the back from his catcher, Sandy Martinez.

him 18 strikeouts for the game. He needed two more to match the record for the most strikeouts in a nine-inning game. The record was held by his boyhood hero, Roger Clemens.

In the ninth inning, Wood struck out the leadoff hitter, Bill Spiers, and then Craig Biggio grounded out. The final batter, Derek Bell, swung and missed at three hard-breaking pitches—he missed the last one by more than a foot. The Cubs won 2–0. The hat Wood wore that day now is on display in the Hall of Fame, but the 20th strikeout ball is not. Wood gave it to his mom.

LEGEND HAS IT

WHO HIT THE LONGEST HOME RUN IN THE HISTORY OF WRIGLEY FIELD?

LEGEND HAS IT that Dave Kingman did. The 6′ 7″ slugger played for the Cubs from 1978 to 1980, but it was as a member of the New York Mets that he made history on a windy day in 1976. Kingman drove a pitch to left-center field that went over the fence, out of the stadium, over Waveland Avenue, and past four houses up Kenmore Avenue. The ball crashed into a third-story porch 550 feet from home plate!

ABOVE: This trading card shows Dave Kingman as a Cub. But he was a Met when he blasted Wrigley's longest homer.

WHO WAS THE CUBS' BEST FOOTBALL PLAYER?

LEGEND HAS IT that Jeff Samardzija was. Samardzija joined the Cubs as a relief pitcher in 2008. Before that, he was a wide receiver for the University of Notre Dame football team. Samardzija caught 77 passes for the Fighting Irish in 2005. A year later, he topped that mark with 78. He graduated with several school records. The Samardzija family was good at a lot of sports. Like Jeff, his brother was a football and baseball star in college. Their father was a professional hockey player.

WHICH CUB PITCHING ACE BEGAN HIS CAREER AS A CATCHING STAR?

LEGEND HAS IT that Carlos Marmol did. Marmol led the team in **saves** in 2010 and 2011. His blazing fastball and quick-moving slider helped him average more than one strikeout per inning. Marmol began throwing the ball from the pitcher's mound to home plate in 2003. Before that, most of his throws went from home plate back to the pitcher. The Cubs originally signed Marmol as a 16-year-old catcher in 1999.

Baseball is a strange game. Sometimes bad teams play well. Other times, great teams play badly. In 1935, Cubs fans weren't sure how to describe their team. Early in the season, the club looked unbeatable at times. Then the Cubs would lose three or four games in a row. This was a big problem, because the St. Louis Cardinals and New York Giants were on a roll. In early July, it looked as if Chicago's season would end without a league championship. The Cubs were more than 10 games out of first place.

The players did not give up. They knew they had tons of talent. The lineup included experienced stars such as Gabby Hartnett, Freddie Lindstrom, Kiki Cuyler, and Chuck Klein. All four would later be voted into the Hall of Fame.

The Cubs had exciting young players, too. Outfielders Augie Galan and Frank Demaree were .300 hitters. Stan Hack, Billy Jurges, Billy Herman, and Phil Cavarretta made up the team's infield. Cavarretta was just 18!

This group gave Chicago fans something to cheer about starting in July. After pulling together, the Cubs won 16 of 17 games.

Gabby Hartnett and pitcher Lon Warneke pose for a photo. Warneke won 20 games for the Cubs in 1935.

Soon, they got back into the pennant race. Still, when they took the field against the Philadelphia Phillies in early September, they remained in third place. What more could a team do?

The Cubs reached down deep and found a little extra magic. On that day in Philadelphia, Galan hit two homers to beat the Phillies. Over the next 23 days, the Cubs played 20 games. Incredibly, they did not lose once during that stretch. Their 21-game September winning streak boosted them into first place. Though the Cubs dropped their last two games, by then it didn't matter—they had already clinched the pennant.

The season had come down to a series against the Cardinals and their famous pitchers, the Dean brothers. Chicago's Lon Warneke beat Paul Dean, and then Bill Lee handed a defeat to Dizzy Dean. The Cardinals, who had won 19 games in September, could only shake their heads as they went home for a long winter as the second-best team in the league.

F or a big-league baseball fan, catching a home run ball is a dream come true. For fans in the bleachers at Wrigley Field, that's only the case if a Cub hits one over the fence. If an enemy batter blasts one into the seats, it's tradition to throw the ball back on the field. That is how much people in Chicago love their Cubs. The fans in the outfield bleachers are so famous for their loyalty that there was a play written about them in the 1970s. Actor Joe Mantegna—a huge Cubs fan—had the original idea. The show is still performed in theaters around the country today.

Another Wrigley Field tradition is the singing of *Take Me Out to the Ballgame* in the seventh inning. For more than 15 years, Harry Caray led the fans in song. The beloved broadcaster announced the games on television and radio. Today there is a statue of Caray outside the ballpark.

LEFT: Harry Caray always made fans smile with his great sense of humor and his love of the Cubs.　　**ABOVE**: This pin was made for fans in 1969 on the day the Cubs honored Billy Williams.

TIMELINE

Frank
Chance

CHANCE-CHICAGO-NAT.

1874
The team plays its first
season as the Chicago
White Stockings.

1907
Frank Chance leads the
Cubs to their first World
Series championship.

1897
Cap Anson retires after 22 years
in a Chicago uniform.

1932
The Cubs win their first of
three pennants in the 1930s.

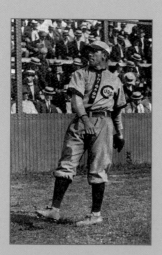

Joe Tinker (left) and
Johnny Evers (right)
were the famous infield
teammates of Frank Chance.

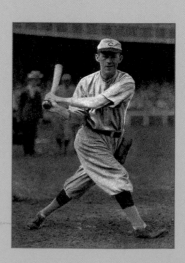

Phil Cavarretta

Bruce Sutter

1945
NL MVP Phil Cavarretta leads the Cubs to the pennant.

1979
Bruce Sutter becomes the second reliever to win the **Cy Young Award**.

1989
The Cubs play in the NLCS for the second time in six years.

1959
Ernie Banks wins his second NL MVP award.

2011
Starlin Castro is an **All-Star** at the age of 21.

Starlin Castro

FUN FACTS

B-A-A-A-A-D LUCK

In Game 4 of the 1945 World Series, the Cubs threw a fan named

Mike Sianis out of the ballpark. He had brought his billygoat, Murphy, for good luck. The angry Sianis put a "curse" on the Cubs. He died 25 years later without lifting it. As of 2011, the Cubs had yet to play in another World Series.

GROUNDBREAKER

In 1962, the Cubs hired Buck O'Neil as a coach. He was the first African-American to hold a big-league coaching job.

RAY OF SUNSHINE

In 1922, Ray Grimes of the Cubs drove in at least one run 17 games in a row. That is still a big-league record.

HARD LESSON

The Cubs were one of the first teams to insist all their players wear batting helmets. The new rule started the day after Ernie Banks—then a **rookie**—was hit in the head by a pitch during spring training in 1954.

SPEECHLESS

In 1905, Joe Tinker and Johnny Evers had an argument over a taxi fare. They did not talk to each other for seven years. During that time, they became the greatest **double-play combination** in Cubs history.

LIGHTS OUT

Wrigley Field was the last ballpark to install lights for night baseball. The Cubs actually bought light towers in the 1940s but donated them to the Navy to help train sailors for *World War II*.

BROTHERS IN ARMS

In 1975, Chicago pitchers Rick and Paul Reuschel beat the Los Angeles Dodgers 7–0. It was the first time in history two brothers teamed up to pitch a shutout.

LEFT: Buck O'Neil   **ABOVE**: Ernie Banks

"No player in baseball history worked harder, suffered more, or did it better than Andre Dawson. He's the best I've ever seen."

▶ **RYNE SANDBERG**, ON HIS TEAMMATE WHO WAS VOTED INTO THE HALL OF FAME IN 2010

"He can run, he can throw, he can hit, and he's smart. He's only going to get better."

▶ **ARAMIS RAMIREZ**, ON THE FUTURE OF STARLIN CASTRO

CUBS

Ron Santo | **3RD BASE**

"I played the game the way it should be played."

▶ **RON SANTO**, ON GIVING HIS ALL EVERY TIME HE TOOK THE FIELD

"I'm living my dream. This is all I ever wanted to do or be."

▶ **KERRY WOOD**, ON THE THRILL OF PLAYING IN THE BIG LEAGUES

"People who come out here are like my friends. People that play here are like my brothers."

▶ **ERNIE BANKS**, *ON HIS 19 YEARS AT WRIGLEY FIELD*

"All I did all my whole life was play hard and give everything I had for the organization and for the people of Chicago."

▶ **SAMMY SOSA**, *ON HIS LOVE FOR THE CUBS AND THEIR FANS*

LEFT: Ron Santo
RIGHT: Sammy Sosa

GREAT DEBATES

Peple who root for the Cubs love to compare their favorite moments, teams, and players. Some debates have been going on for years! How would you settle these classic baseball arguments?

GREG MADDUX WAS THE CUBS GREATEST PITCHER ...

... because he truly mastered the art of pitching. Maddux (LEFT) didn't have an overpowering fastball or curve, but he always found a way to win. He threw the ball where hitters least expected it. He changed speeds and kept them off-balance. Maddux won 20 games with a 2.18 **earned run average (ERA)** in 1992. For a pitcher in Wrigley Field, those were awesome numbers.

WAIT A SECOND! TAKE A LOOK AT THE NUMBERS FERGIE JENKINS HAD ...

... because he pitched in the same ballpark and won 20 games six years in a row! Jenkins was just as much an artist as Maddux was. He had a great fastball and dared batters to hit it. Jenkins could throw a pitch that dipped down at the last instant and another that stayed up high. He made great hitters look like rookies.

HANK SAUER
outfield, Chicago Cubs

WRIGLEY FIELD IS BASEBALL'S BEST BALLPARK ...

… because the game looks the same as it did when your great-grandparents were fans. Tradition is important in baseball, and no stadium has more of it than Wrigley Field. The fans sit so close to the field that they can talk to the players—and the players sometimes talk back. How great is that!

THAT'S GREAT ALL RIGHT, BUT WRIGLEY FIELD MAY ALSO HURT THE CUBS ...

… because it is hard to build a winning team there. When the wind is blowing in one direction, every fly ball has a chance to be a home run. When the wind is blowing in the opposite direction, it is almost impossible to reach the bleachers. Is it better to have power hitters or line-drive hitters in Wrigley? Is it better to have tricky pitchers who make batters hit ground balls, or pitchers who throw hard and get batters to hit the ball in the air? That's the problem. You can't have them all!

T he great Cubs teams and players have left their marks on the record books. These are the "best of the best" …

Ken Hubbs

Fergie Jenkins

CUBS AWARD WINNERS

WINNER	AWARD	YEAR
Rogers Hornsby	Most Valuable Player	1929
Gabby Hartnett	Most Valuable Player	1935
Phil Cavarretta	Most Valuable Player	1945
Hank Sauer	Most Valuable Player	1952
Ernie Banks	Most Valuable Player	1958
Ernie Banks	Most Valuable Player	1959
Billy Williams	Rookie of the Year	1961
Ken Hubbs	Rookie of the Year	1962
Fergie Jenkins	Cy Young Award	1971
Bill Madlock	All-Star Game co-MVP	1975
Bruce Sutter	Cy Young Award	1979
Rick Sutcliffe	Cy Young Award	1984
Ryne Sandberg	Most Valuable Player	1984
Jim Frey	Manager of the Year	1984
Andre Dawson	Most Valuable Player	1987
Jerome Walton	Rookie of the Year	1989
Don Zimmer	Manager of the Year	1989
Greg Maddux	Cy Young Award	1992
Kerry Wood	Rookie of the Year	1998
Sammy Sosa	Most Valuable Player	1998
Geovany Soto	Rookie of the Year	2008

ACHIEVEMENT	YEAR
NL Pennant Winners	1876
NL Pennant Winners	1880
NL Pennant Winners	1881
NL Pennant Winners	1882
NL Pennant Winners	1885
NL Pennant Winners	1886
NL Pennant Winners	1906
NL Pennant Winners	1907
World Series Champions	1907
NL Pennant Winners	1908
World Series Champions	1908
NL Pennant Winners	1910
NL Pennant Winners	1918
NL Pennant Winners	1929
NL Pennant Winners	1932
NL Pennant Winners	1935
NL Pennant Winners	1938
NL Pennant Winners	1945
NL East Champions	1984
NL East Champions	1989
NL Central Champions	2003
NL Central Champions	2007
NL Central Champions	2008

TOP RIGHT: Cap Anson, a member of the Cubs for 22 years, was a part of six pennant-winning teams in the 1800s.

BOTTOM RIGHT: This pin was given to reporters during the 1932 World Series.

PINPOINTS

The history of a baseball team is made up of many smaller stories. These stories take place all over the map—not just in the city a team calls "home." Match the pushpins on these maps to the **TEAM FACTS**, and you will begin to see the story of the Cubs unfold!

1. Chicago, Illinois—*The Cubs have played here since 1874.*
2. Detroit, Michigan—*The Cubs clinched the 1908 World Series here.*
3. Seattle, Washington—*Ron Santo was born here.*
4. Fresno, California—*Frank Chance was born here.*
5. Milwaukee, Wisconsin—*Bill Madlock was named co-MVP of the 1975 All-Star Game here.*
6. Whistler, Alabama—*Billy Williams was born here.*
7. Troy, New York—*Johnny Evers was born here.*
8. Lancaster, Pennsylvania—*Bruce Sutter was born here.*
9. Winston-Salem, North Carolina—*Mark Grace was born here.*
10. Chatham, Ontario, Canada—*Fergie Jenkins was born here.*
11. Monte Cristi, Domincan Replubic—*Starlin Castro was born here.*
12. Puerto Cabella, Venezuela—*Carlos Zambrano was born here.*

Starlin Castro

GLOSSARY

ALL-STAR—A player who is selected to play in baseball's annual All-Star Game.

BIG-LEAGUER—Someone who plays in the major leagues.

BLEACHER SEATS—The seats located beyond the outfield fences, where fans get "bleached" by the sun.

CY YOUNG AWARD—The annual trophy given to each league's best pitcher.

DECADE—A period of 10 years; also specific periods, such as the 1950s.

DOUBLEHEADER—Two games in one day.

DOUBLE-PLAY COMBINATION—A term for a shortstop and second baseman; together, they often turn double-plays.

EARNED RUN AVERAGE (ERA)—A statistic that measures how many runs a pitcher gives up for every nine innings he pitches.

FIERY—Showing strong emotion.

FORCE-OUT—An out made at a base that a runner is forced to advance to.

GRAND SLAM—A home run with the bases loaded.

GRANDSTAND—The sections of seats that make up the tall (or "grand") part of a stadium.

HALL OF FAME—The museum in Cooperstown, New York, where baseball's greatest players are honored.

LEADOFF HITTER—The first hitter in a lineup, or the first hitter in an inning.

MINOR LEAGUES—The many professional leagues that help develop players for the major leagues.

MOST VALUABLE PLAYER (MVP)—The award given each year to each league's top player; an MVP is also selected for the World Series and the All-Star Game.

NATIONAL LEAGUE (NL)—The older of the two major leagues; the NL began play in 1876.

NATIONAL LEAGUE CHAMPIONSHIP SERIES (NLCS)—The playoff series that has decided the NL pennant since 1969.

NL CENTRAL—A group of NL teams that play in the central part of the country.

PENNANT—A league championship. The term comes from the triangular flag awarded to each season's champion, beginning in the 1870s.

PINSTRIPES—Thin stripes.

POSTSEASON—The games played after the regular season, including the playoffs and World Series.

ROOKIE—A player in his first season.

RUNS BATTED IN (RBIs)—A statistic that counts the number of runners a batter drives home.

SAVES—A statistic that counts the number of times a relief pitcher finishes off a close victory for his team.

SHUT OUT—Did not allow an opponent to score. A game won in this way is called a shutout.

TRADITION—A belief or custom that is handed down from generation to generation.

VETERANS—Players who have great experience.

WORLD SERIES—The world championship series played between the American League and National League pennant winners.

WORLD WAR II—The war among the major powers of Europe, Asia, and North America that lasted from 1939 to 1945. The United States entered the war in 1941.

EXTRA INNINGS

TEAM SPIRIT introduces a great way to stay up to date with your team! Visit our **EXTRA INNINGS** link and get connected to the latest and greatest updates. **EXTRA INNINGS** serves as a young reader's ticket to an exclusive web page—with more stories, fun facts, team records, and photos of the Cubs. Content is updated during and after each season. The **EXTRA INNINGS** feature also enables readers to send comments and letters to the author! Log onto:

www.norwoodhousepress.com/library.aspx

and click on the tab: **TEAM SPIRIT** to access **EXTRA INNINGS**.

Read all the books in the series to learn more about professional sports. For a complete listing of the baseball, basketball, football, and hockey teams in the **TEAM SPIRIT** series, visit our website at:

www.norwoodhousepress.com/library.aspx

ON THE ROAD

CHICAGO CUBS
1060 West Addison Street
Chicago, Illinois 60613
(773) 404-2827
chicago.cubs.mlb.com

NATIONAL BASEBALL HALL OF FAME AND MUSEUM
25 Main Street
Cooperstown, New York 13326
(888) 425-5633
www.baseballhalloffame.org

ON THE BOOKSHELF

To learn more about the sport of baseball, look for these books at your library or bookstore:

- Augustyn, Adam (editor). *The Britannica Guide to Baseball*. New York, NY: Rosen Publishing, 2011.

- Dreier, David. *Baseball: How It Works*. North Mankato, MN: Capstone Press, 2010.

- Stewart, Mark. *Ultimate 10: Baseball*. New York, NY: Gareth Stevens Publishing, 2009.

INDEX

PAGE NUMBERS IN **BOLD** REFER TO ILLUSTRATIONS.

ABOUT THE AUTHOR

MARK STEWART has written more than 50 books on baseball and over 150 sports books for kids. He grew up in New York City during the 1960s rooting for the Yankees and Mets, and was lucky enough to meet players from both teams. Mark comes from a family of writers. His grandfather was Sunday Editor of *The New York Times,* and his mother was Articles Editor of *Ladies' Home Journal* and *McCall's*. Mark has profiled hundreds of athletes over the past 25 years. He has also written several books about his native New York and New Jersey, his home today. Mark is a graduate of Duke University, with a degree in history. He lives and works in a home overlooking Sandy Hook, New Jersey. You can contact Mark through the Norwood House Press website.